2004 | Higher

[BLANK]

X010/301

NATIONAL
QUALIFICATIONS
2004

FRIDAY, 4 JUNE
1.00 PM – 3.30 PM

BUSINESS
MANAGEMENT
HIGHER

Candidates should attempt **all** questions in Section **One** and **two** questions from Section **Two**.

Read all the questions carefully.

100 marks are allocated to this paper.

50 marks for Section **One** and

50 marks for Section **Two**.

Answers are to be written in the answer book provided.

SCOTTISH
QUALIFICATIONS
AUTHORITY

SECTION ONE

This section should take you approximately 1 hour 15 minutes.

Read through the following information, then answer the questions which follow.

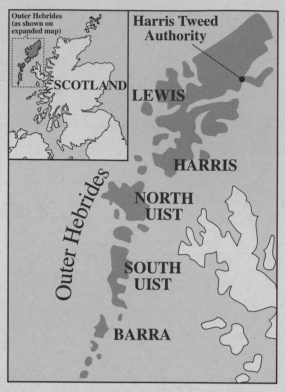

Harris is one of the islands in the Outer Hebrides situated off the North West coast of Scotland.

TWEED FIRM IS PUT ON THE MARKET FOR THE FIRST TIME	**CANDIDATE'S NOTES**

Harris Tweed is the world's only commercially produced handwoven tweed—a woven wool fabric suitable for the manufacture of jackets and suits. Originally the tweed was used to produce hard wearing, warm, water-resistant clothing for sport and outdoor pursuits. More recently it has been used by fashion designers such as Vivienne Westwood, Paul Smith and John Galliano.

The cloth has always been at the "top end" of the fabric market.

THE PROPOSED SALE

Derick Murray is the owner of the KM Group which is responsible for 97% of Harris Tweed's total production. He has decided to sell his business. This threatens the jobs of 70 mill employees and 200 home-based weavers, who use a loom to convert wool into cloth. The reason being given is "purely a personal one". His son is employed in the computer industry and his daughter is at University and about to embark on her own career. This is typical of young people brought up on the islands—they leave the islands to further their education and many choose not to return.

CANDIDATE'S NOTES

THE PRODUCT

Originally the wool, obtained from the island's sheep, was handspun and distributed to weavers who today still work in their own homes where they use weaving looms. The original wooden looms were replaced in 1920, which enabled the weavers to produce more  complicated patterns. This type of loom was used until the 1990s when the interest in Harris Tweed by fashion designers necessitated the production of a softer, lighter and wider fabric. This was made possible by the introduction of more modern double width looms. The cost of these new looms was partly funded by EU and Government grants of £11 million. The rest was paid by the weavers themselves, many of whom borrowed heavily and are still paying off loans. The weavers required training when the new looms were introduced.

The weavers return the cloth to the mill where it is washed and sent to the buyer. The weaving process normally takes 3 days. Mill spun yarn is now used, as opposed to the traditional handspun yarn which has resulted in an increased production rate. A substantial amount of Harris Tweed is exported. For each 80 metres of fabric, the weaver receives £140. It is sold on for about £14 per metre. Weavers are lucky if they make £9,000 per year.

QUALITY STANDARDS

In 1909 the Harris Tweed Authority was established to ensure the cloth was made to the proper standards. Fabric passing the test carries a trademark—an orb and the Maltese Cross—along with "woven in . . .". This prevents competitors from trying to pass off imitations as genuine Harris Tweed.

The product is currently protected by the Harris Tweed Act 1993. It gives the definition of the product as "cloth that has been handwoven by the islanders of Lewis, Harris, Uist and Barra in their own homes". Originally, the cloth had to be produced from the wool of sheep reared on the islands, but as production outstripped the capacity to produce wool, the use of raw materials from other parts of Scotland was allowed.

MARKETING

The late 1990s proved to be a difficult time for the British textile industry generally. Several marketing initiatives took place to try and encourage sales of Harris Tweed, particulary to the Canadian and US markets where the product used to be very popular.

The Scottish Office have played their part too. In January 2001, a brochure in Japanese was launched by Brian Wilson, the Scottish Office Minister, at the International Fashion Fair in Tokyo.

In August 2001, a fashion show was planned as part of "Scotland Week". This was held in Brussels in an attempt to show the fabric and the work of Scottish fashion designers to the European market.

CANDIDATE'S NOTES

THE WEBSITE

The Harris Tweed Authority has its own Web page introduced by the Gaelic Band "Capercaille" singing "Skye Waulking Song". It gives details of the fabric's history and shows samples of the fabric itself. This allows the website visitor to see the pattern details quite clearly. The location of the islands is also made clear with the use of pictures and maps and details of accommodation are provided for potential visitors. An e-mail address is available for those wishing to contact the company.

Searching the Internet allows a browser to find many other sites which offer tweed products for sale—jackets are priced between £105 and £149 with approximately £6·50 charged for overseas postage.

THE FUTURE...

Community leaders are optimistic that the Harris Tweed Act 1993 will protect jobs on the islands.

Labour MSP, Alasdair Morrison, pledged public support to any new owner of the mill who is prepared to guarantee the continuation of its jobs and work for the future of Harris Tweed.

The Transport and General Workers' Union at the KM Group stated "We would be quite happy if a new buyer for the mill is found. A new owner could result in expansion and more jobs."

CANDIDATE'S NOTES

Adapted from *The Herald*, 29 August 2002, *The Mail on Sunday*, 22 September 2002, *www.harristweed.com*

Marks

QUESTIONS

You should note that although the following questions are based on the stimulus material, it does not contain all the information needed to provide suitable answers to all the questions. You will need to make use of knowledge you have acquired whilst studying the course.

Answer ALL the questions.

1. Identify the problems of the Harris Tweed industry, both past and present. You should use the following headings. **10**
   - Human Resources
   - Operations
   - Marketing

2. The weavers required training when new equipment was introduced.
   (*a*) What are the costs and benefits of staff training for an organisation? **6**
   (*b*) Describe and justify an appropriate training method for a manufacturing company such as Harris Tweed. **4**
   (*c*) Describe the means by which Information Communications Technology (ICT) can support training. **6**

3. The Harris Tweed Act is an item of legislation which protects a **product**. Identify and describe 2 forms of legislation which exist in order to protect **employees** in the workplace. **4**

4. Harris Tweed has a trademark. Describe the benefits of holding a trademark or Quality Symbol for
   (i) an organisation
   (ii) the consumer. **4**

5. The employees are one group of Harris Tweed's stakeholders. Describe how 3 other stakeholders can influence organisations. **6**

6. Several marketing initiatives have been used by Harris Tweed.
   (*a*) Discuss the use of the internet in marketing an organisation. **4**
   (*b*) Discuss a pricing tactic likely to be used by an organisation offering an exclusive or unique product. **4**

7. How might a potential buyer of Harris Tweed use ratios calculated from the final accounts? **2**

(50)

[END OF SECTION ONE]

Marks

SECTION TWO

This section should take you approximately 1 hour 15 minutes.

Answer TWO questions.

1. British Airways has chosen to group its business activities by customer (business and private travellers).

    (a) Describe the advantages and disadvantages of this type of grouping. **5**

    (b) The airline has found that some journeys are not making a profit and Head Office has decided to stop operating these routes, at least in the short term.

        (i) What type of decision does this represent? Justify your choice. **2**

        (ii) Describe the advantages and disadvantages of decentralised decision making. **6**

    (c) (i) Identify and describe the factors which might result in a profitable firm facing cash flow problems. **6**

        (ii) How might an organisation resolve these problems? **6**

    (25)

2. Large football clubs and major sporting events such as F1 motor racing depend heavily on sponsorship as a means of funding.

    (a) Describe 3 alternative sources of finance for a large football club, eg Manchester United plc. Justify your choices. **6**

    (b) Why would a company choose to use sponsorship as a means of promotion? **3**

    (c) One F1 team, Jordan, chose to restructure its organisation by delayering.

    Describe, using diagrams, what is meant by the term "delayering" and the effects it can have on an organisation. **7**

    (d) A sports goods manufacturer is considering introducing a new range of trainers.

        (i) Describe and justify 3 methods of field research which would tell them whether or not this proposal is viable. **6**

        (ii) Describe the difference between random and quota sampling. **2**

        (iii) The manufacturer chose quota sampling rather than random sampling when conducting the research. Justify the choice of quota sampling. **1**

    (25)

Marks

3. (*a*) Discuss the factors to be considered when a large secondary school is selecting a new supplier for its school uniform. **6**

   (*b*) (i) Describe the production method you think the manufacturer would most likely use for the production of these uniforms. Justify your choice. **2**

   (ii) What are the advantages and disadvantages of the method you have chosen? **4**

   (*c*) A manufacturer may choose to supply to customers directly. Discuss the advantages and disadvantages of doing this compared with supplying to

   (i) retailers

   (ii) wholesalers

   for both the manufacturer and the customer. **8**

   (*d*) (i) Explain the term "corporate culture". **1**

   (ii) What advantages might a "corporate culture" bring to an organisation and its employees? **4**

   (25)

4. When choosing a summer holiday, consumers depend largely on information obtained from brochures, television programmes and the Internet.

   (*a*) Discuss the reliability and value of the information which is available to holiday consumers. **8**

   (*b*) Describe 2 suitable types of information required by someone selecting a holiday. Justify your choices. **4**

   (*c*) Identify and describe 2 appropriate methods of promotion for summer holidays. **4**

   (*d*) A company may have the strategic objective to increase its market share by 10% in 2004.

   (i) Describe the internal and external factors which may prevent the achievement of this objective. **6**

   (ii) How might an organisation judge whether the decisions taken to achieve any of its objectives have been the correct ones? **3**

   (25)

5. Nestlé and Cadbury have attempted to take over an American chocolate firm.

   (*a*) (i) This takeover is an example of horizontal integration. Identify and describe 2 alternative methods of growth. **4**

   (ii) Why might growth be an objective for a firm? **4**

   (*b*) (i) Nestlé is an example of a firm which has an extensive "product portfolio". Define this term and discuss the benefits it offers to an organisation. A diagram should be used to support your answer. **8**

   (ii) How can an organisation such as Nestlé ensure each product remains competitive? **4**

   (*c*) Organisations may choose to assess their strengths, weaknesses, opportunities and threats before making important decisions.

   Describe the costs and benefits of using a SWOT analysis in decision making. **5**

   (25)

[END OF QUESTION PAPER]

[BLANK PAGE]

[BLANK]

X010/301

NATIONAL
QUALIFICATIONS
2005

FRIDAY, 3 JUNE
1.00 PM – 3.30 PM

BUSINESS
MANAGEMENT
HIGHER

Candidates should attempt **all** questions in Section **One** and **two** questions from Section **Two**.

Read all the questions carefully.

100 marks are allocated to this paper.

50 marks for Section **One** and

50 marks for Section **Two**.

Answers are to be written in the answer book provided.

SCOTTISH
QUALIFICATIONS
AUTHORITY

©

SECTION ONE

This section should take you approximately 1 hour 15 minutes.

Read through the following information, then answer the questions which follow.

THE SCOTTISH FISHING INDUSTRY

Fishing is part of the primary business sector. Fish caught are sold to hotels, supermarkets, fish shops and of course provide the fish and chip shops with one of its most important raw materials.

In Fraserburgh huge fishing boats, known as trawlers, go out to sea for trips which may last up to 10 days. Each trawler is worth over £600,000 and many have been financed by a bank loan. Storms can result in very expensive repair bills.

CANDIDATE'S NOTES

THREATS TO THE WHITE FISH BUSINESS

There are currently 455 boats registered to catch cod and haddock. The majority of these boats are based in North-East Scotland and provide 1315 jobs.

In order to preserve declining fish stocks, the EU (European Union) has restricted the number of fishing days allowed to 15 per month. The amount caught must be reduced by almost 50%. The Scottish Executive announced a £50 million compensation deal for those willing to decommission (scrap) their vessels. The effect on fishing communities is extensive, leaving many workers demoralised.

The fishing crews express concern that some of the other EU countries continue to fish off the Scottish coast. Some of them also believe that the shortage of cod is not a result of overfishing, as claimed by the EU, but has been caused by a rise in the temperature of the water.

Fish farming, where fish are bred in cages, in sea lochs, is an alternative way of supplying the market. However, some argue that the quality of the fish is poorer than the cod caught in the sea. Environmentalists are also concerned that waste products from fish farming result in increased levels of water pollution.

OPERATIONS

At sea, the trawlers become floating factories. Sonar devices enable the crews to track fish. Enormous fishing nets are lifted on board by a mechanical device, hopefully heavy with fish. Some of the crew work below deck, at a conveyor belt, cleaning the fish. The fish are then passed down a tube into a steel cold-storage tank. The crew sort the fish into boxes by type and size, using ice to keep it fresh.

Fishing restrictions affect other businesses too: one box supplier is being forced to diversify and has started producing plant boxes for garden centres.

It is estimated that each ten-day trip costs £13,000 per boat. The profits are shared between the crew. It is possible for each member of the crew to earn £1,600 per trip. If the catch is small then the wages are low. The fish is auctioned in a fish market. High quality fish is obviously the most popular with the buyers and commands the highest price. Shortages of cod mean that consumers face high prices and they may well choose alternative products.

CANDIDATE'S NOTES

LEGISLATION

Fishing boat skippers must keep records of quantities of fish caught. Government patrol boats may demand to see these records. The fishing authorities might also check that the size of the net is legal—smaller holes in the nets prevent young fish from escaping back to their breeding grounds. The crew may be fined tens of thousands of pounds for breaking these rules.

TRAINING

Traditionally, boys brought up in fishing towns joined their fathers at sea where the skills were passed on. Banff and Buchan College provides training in fishing skills, but last year no one applied for the course. Only a few years ago 45 people would normally train each year. Highly paid jobs in the oil industry appear more attractive to younger people.

PROTECTING A TRADEMARK	CANDIDATE'S NOTES
Several miles down the North East coast, another fish processing business faces a different problem. There is a campaign to protect the identity of the "Arbroath Smokie"—smoked haddock. If successful it would mean the product, promoted as a regional delicacy, could not be produced or packaged without coming specifically from the Arbroath area–the name therefore would become a trademark. Registration of the trade name would protect the product from cheap imitations, preserving its reputation as a high quality product.	

Adapted from *Sunday Herald*, 4 and 11 May 2003, *Dundee Courier*, 21 May 2003

Marks

QUESTIONS

You should note that although the following questions are based on the stimulus material, it does not contain all the information needed to provide suitable answers to all the questions. You will need to make use of knowledge you have acquired whilst studying the course.

Answer ALL the questions.

1. Identify the **problems** faced by Scottish fishing businesses. Use the following headings. (Please identify problems only, solutions will not be credited.)   **10**
    - Human Resources
    - Marketing
    - Finance
    - Operations

2. Cutting quotas (the amount of fish which fishing crews are allowed to catch) will mean that fish shops will have difficulty in obtaining sufficient stocks of cod to meet the needs of their customers.

    (*a*) For any organisation, describe the problems of

       (i) understocking

      (ii) overstocking.   **6**

    (*b*) Explain how ICT (Information Communications Technology) can help stock control management (eg in supermarkets).   **4**

3. The article suggests that fishing crews are trained both **on the job** and **off the job**.

    (*a*) Describe each of these types of training.   **2**

    (*b*) Discuss the costs and benefits of training staff.   **6**

4. (*a*) Loans are required to purchase the fishing boats. Describe and justify 2 other sources of finance available to organisations who wish to make large capital investments.   **4**

    (*b*) Once the boat owners have covered all their costs, the amount remaining from the sale of the fish is known as profit.

    Identify 2 ratios which can be used to measure the profitability/performance of an organisation and explain why they should **not** be the only measure of its success.   **6**

5. Wholesalers are responsible for purchasing fish in bulk from the fish market. Explain the role of a wholesaler.   **4**

[Turn over

Marks

6. Modern technology allows fishing crews to obtain up-to-date information about the location of fish, enabling them to make the decision as to the best place to operate.

    (*a*) Describe the value and reliability of

      (i) primary, and

      (ii) secondary information for organisations.   **4**

    (*b*) Explain factors which may influence the quality of a decision.   **4**

                                                          (50)

[END OF SECTION ONE]

Marks

SECTION TWO

This section should take you approximately 1 hour 15 minutes.

Answer TWO questions.

1. A local entrepreneur decides to set up a business.

   (*a*) Identify 4 organisations which offer advice to someone setting up in business. **4**

   (*b*) (i) Explain how ICT (Information Communications Technology) could support an organisation in the areas of

   - marketing
   - human resources
   - finance. **5**

   (ii) Outline factors which might restrict the use of technology. **4**

   (*c*) Describe 3 forms of legislation which would affect the running of an organisation. **6**

   (*d*) Describe and explain the purpose of the following when recruiting new staff. **6**

   - Job description
   - Person specification
   - Reference

   (25)

2. Some organisations are changing their working practices, for example, introducing flexible working and homeworking.

   (*a*) Describe the possible benefits of these changes to working practices for

   - the employee
   - the employer. **4**

   (*b*) An organisation may choose to "downsize" and "outsource". Describe the meaning of these terms and the consequences for an organisation. **7**

   (*c*) (i) Describe the advantages and disadvantages of a centralised organisation structure. **6**

   (ii) Explain what is meant by a "matrix structure". **2**

   (*d*) Employees may choose to take industrial action when they cannot agree on certain issues with their employer.

   (i) Describe 2 forms of industrial action and an affect each action could have on an organisation. **4**

   (ii) Describe the contents and purpose of a written disciplinary procedure. **2**

   (25)

[Turn over

Marks

3. Many companies selling branded goods (eg Levi and Pepsi-Cola) are moving into new markets such as China.

   (*a*) Describe the benefits of holding a brand name. 4

   (*b*) (i) Companies operating in different geographical areas may choose to group their activities by territory. Describe an advantage and a disadvantage of doing so. 2

   (ii) Discuss 2 other types of activity grouping. 4

   (*c*) Levi and Pepsi-Cola's move into a new market is an example of growth.

   Describe other methods of growth. 6

   (*d*) Explain some of the measures companies take to ensure their products are of a high quality. 9

   (25)

4. (*a*) Describe the importance of Research and Development to an organisation. 4

   (*b*) (i) Shareholders are one of the company's stakeholders. Explain why shareholders are interested in an organisation's financial information. 4

   (ii) Describe how 5 other stakeholders could **influence** an organisation. 5

   (*c*) Give one example each of a strategic, tactical and operational decision taken by an organisation. 3

   (*d*) (i) Describe the advantages and disadvantages to an organisation of using a structured decision-making model. 6

   (ii) State how a Director would know that a decision taken was effective. 3

   (25)

5. Mobile phone operators have been criticised for overcharging customers and may be forced by legislation to reduce their prices.

   (*a*) Describe 4 factors which allow organisations to remain successful while charging customers high prices. 4

   (*b*) (i) Identify 2 objectives of firms operating in a highly competitive market such as the mobile phone industry. 2

   (ii) Describe pricing strategies which could be used to achieve these objectives. 4

   (*c*) (i) Explain why organisations choose to spend large sums of money on marketing. 5

   (ii) Other than altering prices, describe 2 methods of promotion which are used by organisations. 2

   (*d*) Profitable firms may fail due to poor cash flow.

   Identify 4 sources of cash flow problems and suggest one solution for each source you have identified. 8

   (25)

[END OF QUESTION PAPER]

[BLANK PAGE]

X010/301

NATIONAL
QUALIFICATIONS
2006

THURSDAY, 18 MAY
1.00 PM – 3.30 PM

BUSINESS
MANAGEMENT
HIGHER

Candidates should attempt **all** questions in Section **One** and **two** questions from Section **Two**.

Read all the questions carefully.

100 marks are allocated to this paper.

50 marks for Section **One** and

50 marks for Section **Two**.

Answers are to be written in the answer book provided.

SCOTTISH
QUALIFICATIONS
AUTHORITY

SECTION ONE

This section should take you approximately 1 hour 15 minutes.

Read through the following information, then answer the questions which follow.

	CANDIDATE'S NOTES

GOING DOWNHILL

DIFFICULTIES OF SCOTTISH SKIING

New operators are being sought for 2 of Scotland's best known ski centres, Glenshee and Glencoe. Glenshee is located in the popular tourist area of Royal Deeside, where the Queen's summer residence, Balmoral Castle, is located. A management team has placed a bid to purchase the loss-making Glenshee Centre.

Snow and skiers are thin on the ground these days. In November it was announced that the Glencoe resort would close for the winter. Global warming and cheap flights to Alpine resorts are partly to blame. Since the late 1980s the number of days with sufficient snow for skiing has fallen by about a quarter. Ironically, when it does snow the roads are blocked, making it impossible to reach the slopes. One local school cancelled a planned 2–day ski trip due to lack of snow, only to face closure of the whole school a few days later because of heavy snow.

The US dollar ($) is weak against the £ at the moment. This makes visiting Scotland expensive for American tourists. The exchange rate does work in the Scottish skier's favour however, as travelling to the North American slopes appears a much more attractive option.

Jeremy Clarkson, writing in The Sunday Times, expresses the opinion that skiing in Scotland lacks the image of Europe. He states that "skiing in Scotand is like learning to scuba dive in a quarry". Others would dispute his view. He does point out, however, that travelling to Scotland is no easier than to Europe for those living in the South of England.

COSTS

Skiing is an expensive sport. Those not owning their own equipment can hire skis for approximately £16 per day and ski-suits for £11 per day. A lift pass will cost £22 per day although a 50% discount is offered to beginners. Training costs £12 for 2 hours although again package deals are available. Other promotional deals are available such as an "Advantage Card" which can be purchased for £40 and entitles the holder to 40% off lift passes for the season. A seasonal pass costs £180.

THE WEBSITE

The ski resorts have their own websites, describing how to get there and listing accommodation details. Up-to-date information regarding skiing conditions is available, along with reviews of the resorts. There are links to ski-shops, enabling people to purchase skiing equipment. It is also possible to order resort brochures on-line.

CANDIDATE'S NOTES

DEVELOPING THE PRODUCT

Scottish Skiing is heavily subsidised. £27 million in Government aid has been granted to the industry in the past 15 years.

In the mid 1990s Highlands and Islands Enterprise decided one other resort, Cairngorm, needed a makeover. A decision was taken to replace the chairlift (the means by which skiers reach the top of the slopes) with a funicular railway, at an estimated cost of £14·8 million. This went £4·8 million over-budget because the construction proved to be a very complicated engineering process. This had to be funded by the taxpayer.

Conservationists had been partly to blame for the overspend by delaying the work for one year. They protested that rare plants and birds would be destroyed by the plan. The work itself and the prospect in the long term of numerous tourists walking over the area upset them.

The funicular railway is only part of Cairngorm's development. A restaurant, mountain exhibition and shop also exist. Marked footpaths allow walking and mountain biking to take place in the area now designated a National Park. A golf course was also purchased by the owners of the Glenshee Ski Centre in order to provide income all year round as skiing is such a seasonal sport.

[Turn over

FINANCE

Cairngorm has been losing money since 1998 (£1·9 million in 2002) and the extra 150,000 visitors brought by the funicular railway has not been enough to make the enterprise profitable. The company could break even if  its workforce of 85 permanent and 200 seasonal workers was cut. However, the European Union gave £2·7 million towards the railway on the understanding that jobs would be created, so making people redundant would be impossible without paying the grant back.

Criticism has been made generally of the Scottish Executive's attitude to tourism. It has been suggested that an additional investment of £20 million would give a boost to the Scottish economy of £2 billion a year. The areas of Glenshee and Cairngorm are heavily dependent on tourism.

CANDIDATE'S NOTES

Adapted from *The Courier*, 14 February 2004, *www.thisisnorthscotland.co.uk*, *www.economist.com*, *www.timesonline.co.uk*

Marks

QUESTIONS

You should note that although the following questions are based on the stimulus material, it does not contain all the information needed to provide suitable answers to all the questions. You will need to make use of knowledge you have acquired whilst studying the course.

Answer ALL the questions.

1. Identify the problems of the Scottish skiing industry. You should use the following headings. (Please identify problems only, solutions will not be credited.) **10**
   - Marketing
   - Operations
   - Finance
   - External Factors

2. A newspaper article stated that "Scotland lacks the image of Europe".
   (*a*) Describe **3** methods of promoting Scotland's tourist industry. **3**
   (*b*) Discuss the value and reliabilty of
      (i) primary information
      (ii) secondary information. **6**

3. "Skiing is an expensive sport."
   (*a*) Describe a pricing tactic which could be used to ensure a new product or service appears exclusive. **2**
   (*b*) Contrast this with a pricing tactic which could be used by a firm in a highly competitive market. **2**

4. The skiing industry, like many other organisations, has its own website.
   (*a*) Describe the advantages to an organisation of having a website. **6**
   (*b*) Describe **2** measures organisations can use to encourage customers to purchase from their website. **2**
   (*c*) Describe **2** types of information contained in a typical website. **2**

5. (*a*) Government aid helped finance the new developments. Describe and justify **2** other sources of long term finance which could be chosen by firms undertaking such large scale developments. **4**
   (*b*) The developments meant the product portfolio was extended. Describe the benefits of holding a varied product portfolio. **5**

6. The organisation overspent its budget. Outline the reasons for preparing budgets. **5**

7. Discuss what makes one pressure group more effective than another. **3**

(50)

[END OF SECTION ONE]

[Turn over

Marks

SECTION TWO

This section should take you approximately 1 hour 15 minutes.

Answer TWO questions.

1. A local restaurant which has a capacity to hold 50 customers finds it frequently has fewer than 5 customers. The problems have been identified as poor quality and overpriced food.

   (a) Describe the benefits of using a decision making model in order to solve problems. **5**

   (b) (i) Explain the factors which are important in selecting an appropriate supplier of raw materials for the restaurant. **5**

       (ii) Describe other means by which quality food and service can be guaranteed at all times. **6**

   (c) Describe a selection process which may be used to ensure the best applicants are appointed to work in the restaurant. **5**

   (d) Discuss the value of an appraisal system. **4**

   (25)

2. (a) Describe the factors affecting an organisation's choice of channel of distribution. **7**

   (b) (i) Customers provide organisations with personal information. Explain the ways in which organisations can use this to their advantage. **4**

       (ii) Describe legislation which protects consumers from misuse of information held about them. **6**

   (c) Discuss the effects of introducing new technology on organisations. **8**

   (25)

3. (a) (i) Discuss the objectives of a plc compared to those of a public sector organisation. **5**

       (ii) Describe, using examples, the **3** types of decisions taken by organisations in order to achieve their objectives. **6**

   (b) (i) Discuss the importance of the Annual Accounts in showing whether or not an organisation has achieved its objectives. **4**

       (ii) Describe one interest each of the following stakeholders has in an organisation's information.

        • Inland Revenue

        • Employees

        • Creditors **3**

   (c) Explain the advantages of franchising for a franchiser. **3**

   (d) Describe the advantages and disadvantages of branding to an organisation. **4**

   (25)

Marks

4. Zara, a Spanish fashion store, keep their stock levels low and restock every 2–3 weeks.

   (*a*) Describe the risks to an organisation running with low stock levels.

   4

   (*b*) (i) Describe what is meant by the term "just in time stock control" and explain its advantages.

   4

   (ii) Discuss the factors which must be taken into account when setting a stock reorder level.

   4

   (*c*) Local managers are "empowered" to make decisions.

   Describe the advantages and disadvantages of decentralised decision making.

   6

   (*d*) A large department store is finding it difficult to maintain profits. A hostile takeover has been proposed by one of its competitors. Shareholders have been offered the opportunity to sell their shares.

   (i) Describe the ways in which shareholders influence organisations.

   3

   (ii) Explain the reasons why a competitor might wish to take over a firm which is not making a great deal of profit.

   4

   (25)

5. (*a*) (i) Employment legislation exists to protect workers.

   Describe the purpose of the

   • Health and Safety at Work Act 1974

   • Race Relations Act 1976

   • Equal Pay Act 1970.

   3

   (ii) Legislation is one example of a **political external** influence. Describe **3** other examples of external influence on an organisation.

   3

   (*b*) Describe the role of each of the following in supporting employees and employers when disputes occur in the workplace.

   (i) Trade Unions

   (ii) ACAS

   6

   (*c*) One method of grouping staff and work within an organisational structure is by product/service.

   Describe the advantages and disadvantages of product/service grouping.

   5

   (*d*) Many organisations choose to outsource their catering service. Describe the advantages and disadvantages of outsourcing.

   8

   (25)

[END OF QUESTION PAPER]

[BLANK PAGE]

[BLANK PAGE]

X234/301

NATIONAL
QUALIFICATIONS
2007

MONDAY, 14 MAY
1.00 PM – 3.30 PM

BUSINESS
MANAGEMENT
HIGHER

Candidates should attempt **all** questions in Section **One** and **two** questions from Section **Two**.

Read all the questions carefully.

100 marks are allocated to this paper.

50 marks for Section **One** and

50 marks for Section **Two**.

Answers are to be written in the answer book provided.

SCOTTISH
QUALIFICATIONS
AUTHORITY

©

SECTION ONE

This section should take you approximately 1 hour 15 minutes.

Read through the following information, then answer the questions which follow.

OBAN HARBOURING FEARS OVER TOURISM

THE PAST

Thirty years ago the police used to stop throngs of tourists at Connel advising them that there was not a bed to be had in Oban, the famous Scottish coastal resort, just a few miles further on. Oban's stake in the tourist business was based on its harbour and the surrounding islands.

There are huge hotels along the beachfront and cruise ships and yachts used to fill the

bay. It became the main point of departure for many of the islands and trips to Iona and Staffa were promoted. These trips were very popular with tourists. Caledonian MacBrayne operated ferries from Oban to Mull and other islands off the West Coast of Scotland. Many large bus tour operators frequently stopped in the town.

THE PRESENT

There are now major concerns amongst local business people that the town's main asset, its waterfront, is not being properly utilised. It is claimed that despite being the natural centre for yachting in Scotland, Oban is missing out on the lucrative trade from yachters because of a lack of vision from the local council. It is felt that not enough is being done to attract tourists from the UK and worldwide; much more promotion needs to be carried out. Oban also has a severe lack of car parking facilities and access to the North Pier is very difficult for cars and buses.

Local business leaders agree it is a disgrace that Oban's harbour has nowhere for yachters to tie up, walk ashore and spend their money. This could be worth £15 million a year to the Highlands and Islands.

OBAN YACHTS

Tony Cox, of Oban Yachts, based on Kerrera provides 56 fully serviced berths with a marine repair and maintenance service, plus a ferry to Oban. Although he is busy, he believes his business and Oban could be even busier. There are only half a dozen moorings in Oban itself. This means Oban loses out on yachters, who spend their money at nearby Dunstaffnage and Ardfern, which can take about 140 yachts each.

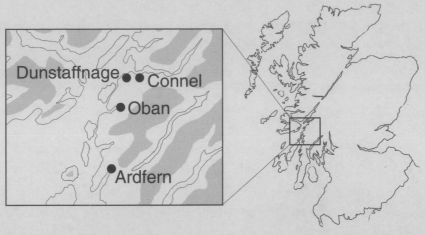

Oban Yachts brings over £300,000 into the local economy each month during the summer season. Tony Cox has invested over £750,000 into Oban Yachts over the last 3 years. However, until he sees action from the local council he is unwilling, like many other local businesses, to invest more money. Tony also has difficulties as he is never certain when busy spells can occur and has to rely on the goodwill of staff to work longer hours at short notice.

EEUSK RESTAURANT

Alan MacLeod, who runs "The Eeusk Restaurant" on the North Pier, is also concerned for the future of tourism in Oban. He feels that there needs to be more attractions to entertain the tourists. Alan insists this would help reduce unemployment in the area, however, there is a lack of experienced workers in Oban. Few people want to work in the tourist industry as it mainly provides seasonal work. Staff are given short term contracts which make the jobs in restaurants and hotels less appealing. Most of the staff in Alan's restaurant are students or part-time workers resulting in a high staff turnover. Alan frequently needs to provide training for the new employees which can be costly.

LOCAL COUNCIL

The local council is taking steps to improve the facilities in Oban. The North Pier is to be developed to include new toilet and showering facilities, with tourists in mind. New restaurants are also planned for the North Pier. The local council is carrying out consultation with stakeholders in an attempt to highlight problems which may have been overlooked.

[Turn over

OTHER ISSUES

One factor that the local council cannot overcome is the weather. The West of Scotland is notorious for rainy, wet summers. This does not appeal to tourists and many people prefer to holiday in a warmer climate. This is a proven stumbling block as with any spell of hot weather the number of visitors to Oban increases. During the warm spell in July and August 2005, the Tourist Information Centre reported that record numbers were visiting the Centre, over 6,200 in one day alone. Many of these tourists were trying to find somewhere to stay and Oban was back to the good times, with not a bed to be found in any hotel or bed and breakfast establishment!

With the drop in tourism over the past few years, linked specially to the lack of American visitors, due to the rise in terrorism in Europe, it is difficult for local businesses to

survive. Hopefully, Oban can again become the place to visit during the summer months. The local business community would certainly flourish as attractions, such as McCaig's Folly, Gylen Castle on Kerrera and the Argyllshire Gathering are second to none.

Adapted from an article in *The Herald*, 28 August 2005, by David Ross

Marks

QUESTIONS

You should note that although the following questions are based on the stimulus material, it does not contain all the information needed to provide suitable answers to all the questions. You will need to make use of knowledge you have acquired whilst studying the course.

Answer ALL the questions.

1. Identify the problems of the Tourist Industry in Oban. You should use the following headings. (Please identify problems only, solutions will not be credited.)
   - Marketing
   - Finance
   - Human Resources
   - External Factors   10

2. The local council are carrying out a consultation exercise with stakeholders. Describe how **4** different stakeholders of the local council could influence the council's future plans.   4

3. Alan MacLeod, the owner of The Eeusk Restaurant, is an entrepreneur. Describe the role of an entrepreneur in a business.   4

4. A gap in the tourist market for yachters exists in Oban. Tony Cox, owner of Oban Yachts, could attempt to target this market.
   (a) Explain the term niche marketing.   2
   (b) The local council are trying to attract tourists to Oban with worldwide marketing of the area. They will need to consider many external factors that could influence the industry.

   Describe external factors that could influence the effectiveness of a marketing campaign.   6

5. (a) Explain why firms can have a healthy profit but experience cash flow problems.   4
   (b) Describe how an organisation could make use of:
   - a production budget
   - a sales budget.   4

6. (a) Describe the changing patterns of employment that have occurred in the UK during the past 20 years.   4
   (b) The Eeusk Restaurant has a problem with high staff turnover. This requires frequent induction training.
   (i) Describe the term induction training.   1
   (ii) Outline the benefits of induction training.   4

Marks

SECTION ONE (continued)

7. Some organisations use a flat rate system to pay employees. Describe other types of payment systems.

    4

8. Many organisations choose to delayer. Explain the benefits of delayering to an organisation.

    3

    (50)

[END OF SECTION ONE]

SECTION TWO

This section should take you approximately 1 hour 15 minutes.

Answer TWO questions.

Marks

1. (*a*) Organisations continually try to obtain primary information about the market in which they operate.

   Describe the advantages and disadvantages of **3** types of field research an organisation could use to obtain primary information.   **8**

   (*b*) Explain the various means of sampling that could be used to obtain a cross section of views when carrying out market research.   **4**

   (*c*) (i) Discuss the ways in which divestment and demerger can assist the growth of an organisation.   **4**

       (ii) Describe other methods of growth.   **5**

   (*d*) Describe how organisations such as The Prince's Trust, banks and Local Enterprise Agencies could provide assistance to a new business.   **4**

     (25)

2. Organisations group their activities in a number of different ways.

   (*a*) Distinguish between the following **3** types of organisational groupings:

   - Product/Service Grouping
   - Customer Grouping
   - Technological Grouping.   **9**

   (*b*) Public sector organisations are owned and controlled by Central Government.

     (i) Describe **2** strategic objectives of a public sector organisation.   **2**

     (ii) Identify **2** sources of funding for a public sector organisation.   **2**

   (*c*) Employee Representative Groups, (eg Trade Unions) use the power of collective bargaining for the benefit of their members. Describe **3** advantages of collective bargaining.   **3**

   (*d*) Various forms of testing are now being used by organisations to ensure the best candidates are selected for a job vacancy.

   Discuss the different types of testing that an organisation could use to select the best candidate.   **6**

   (*e*) Describe the benefits to an organisation of having a strong corporate culture.   **3**

     (25)

3. (*a*) Distinguish between the following financial terms.

   - Gross Profit and Net Profit
   - Fixed Assets and Current Assets
   - Debentures and Shares   **6**

[Turn over

Marks

3. **(continued)**

   (*b*) (i) Describe the main features of the following legislation.

- Health and Safety at Work Act 1974
- Data Protection Act 1984
- Computer Misuse Act 1990   **5**

        (ii) Explain the impact of The Freedom of Information Act 2002 on an organisation.   **2**

   (*c*) Manufacturers use short term promotional measures to boost sales of products or services to retailers (into the pipeline promotions). Identify and describe **2** of these measures.   **4**

   (*d*) Discuss different forms of direct selling available to organisations.   **8**

                (25)

4. Managers try to make effective decisions.

   (*a*) Describe internal constraints that can make decision making difficult.   **6**

   (*b*) Describe ways of using ICT to help decision making.   **6**

   (*c*) Discuss the advantages and disadvantages of a centralised stock control system.   **6**

   (*d*) (i) Describe and justify the use of the following methods of production.

- Job
- Flow   **4**

        (ii) Justify the choice of the following methods of transporting goods.

- Road
- Rail
- Air   **3**

                (25)

5. For firms to survive in the market place they must provide quality products and services.

   (*a*) Explain measures organisations can take to ensure they produce a quality product or service.   **9**

   (*b*) Product endorsement is when firms pay famous people to promote their product or service. Describe the advantages and disadvantages of product endorsement.   **5**

   (*c*) Distinguish between a strategic and tactical decision and give an example of each.   **6**

   (*d*) Firms use ratios to analyse their Annual Accounts.

      (i) Describe reasons for using ratios to analyse performance.   **2**

      (ii) Explain the limitations of ratio analysis.   **3**

                (25)

[END OF QUESTION PAPER]

[BLANK PAGE]

X234/301

NATIONAL
QUALIFICATIONS
2008

WEDNESDAY, 14 MAY
9.00 AM – 11.30 AM

BUSINESS
MANAGEMENT
HiGHER

Candidates should attempt **all** questions in Section **One** and **two** questions from Section **Two**

Read all the questions carefully.

100 marks are allocated to this paper.

50 marks for Section **One** and

50 marks for Section **Two**.

Answers are to be written in the answer book provided.

SECTION ONE

This section should take you approximately 1 hour 15 minutes.

Read through the following information, then answer the questions which follow.

SWEET TASTE OF SUCCESS SPOILED BY SUPERMARKETS

Background

Lees' main business is the manufacture of confectionery and bakery products. It can trace its roots back to 1931, when confectioner John Justice Lees allegedly botched the formula for making a chocolate fondant bar and threw coconut over it in disgust, producing the first macaroon bar. Its customers include major food retailers, food service and catering companies and other food manufacturers. It operates from 2 modern manufacturing sites in Coatbridge and Cambuslang. Lees now employs 155 staff at its Coatbridge plant, along with around 60 at the Waverley Bakery in Cambuslang, which Lees acquired for £600,000 at the beginning of 2003. Macaroon bars and snowballs have been adored by Scots for 75 years—but Lees was going nowhere until former Bell's whisky boss Raymond Miquel became Managing Director and saved the company from bankruptcy.

In recent times supermarkets have put the squeeze on Lees, but the snowball maker still plans to enter more overseas markets and expand through takeover bids. Increases in labour, transport and raw material costs cannot be passed on to consumers because of cut-throat price discounting among the major supermarket chains. Raymond Miquel said "The multiple retailers just won't accept price rises and haven't done for several years, which means we have to keep looking to new markets and new products."

The company experienced some bad times in the 1980s when sales dropped to an all time low. In 1993, the company had a balance sheet worth £350,000 and almost folded with debts of over £5 million owed to suppliers, the Clydesdale Bank and the Inland Revenue. The economic situation at the time didn't help with a worldwide recession. However, they have turned themselves around and built a new factory. Now the products are not only doing well in Scotland but are being sold in the USA, the Netherlands and Ireland. Even the King of Tonga can't get enough of them! This has resulted in a number of supermarkets and confectioners running out of stock of Lees Macaroon Bars as the company has had problems coping with increased demand.

Modernisation and transformation

Miquel saved Lees from liquidation in 1993 when he acquired the company from Northumbrian Fine Food for around £1 million. In 1993, Lees had a number of unprofitable product lines which were eventually shed by Miquel. In the 12 intervening years, however, the company has transformed itself—announcing in 2005 a rise in annual profits of 5 per cent and sales up by 9 per cent. In comparison, in 2002, the company saw sales rise but profits fall.

Miquel, by his own admission, inherited 2 run-down factories producing a handful of old-fashioned products and a very nervous workforce who were concerned for the future of their jobs. Miquel felt that many of the operations aspects of the business were in a

mess. His first decision was to tackle the firm's unprofitability. Many senior managers were not performing to the standards that Miquel expected and as a result were dismissed from their posts. Next to be targeted by Miquel was the outdated 1930s style packaging. Despite working hard, the sales staff were not making enough of a profit margin for the company. This was addressed by recruiting new sales staff and training existing staff.

Miquel describes his style of management as "a bit more hard nosed" than most managing directors and this has caused conflict with some of the long term managers at Lees.

The present situation

Since Miquel took control, sales of macaroon bars have surged, and Lees now sells 2·5 million every year. This represents more than 40 per cent of the company's total confectionery sales. No less popular are Lees snowballs, now selling more than 50 million a year in the UK.

Today Lees is sitting on a massive £6 million in reserve, has no debt and a large overdraft facility. It plans to expand the business overseas and to target other businesses for takeover. Miquel forecasts all kinds of possibilities to diversify, such as restaurants, upmarket tearooms and retail outlets. However, Miquel believes this will be a relatively slow process. Lees will only acquire companies which will add to their profitability, giving them further opportunities to expand in the food industry.

Lees has now floated on the stock market, just over a decade after it stared liquidation in the face. It can only be a matter of time before Miquel's Lees story amazes further!

Adapted from *http://thescotsman.com/business/*

Marks

QUESTIONS

You should note that although the following questions are based on the stimulus material, it does not contain all the information needed to provide suitable answers to all the questions. You will need to make use of knowledge you have acquired whilst studying the course.

Answer ALL the questions.

1. Identify the problems faced by Lees. You should use the following headings. (Please identify problems only, solutions will not be credited.)
   - Marketing
   - Human Resource Management
   - Finance
   - Operations   **10**

2. Organisations often use an entrepreneurial structure. Explain the advantages and disadvantages of an entrepreneurial structure.   **4**

3. Lees could use the Internet to market their brand name to overseas customers.

   Describe the benefits of using the Internet to market products.   **5**

4. Lees' Board of Directors has identified growth as a strategic objective.
   (a) Explain internal factors which could be taken into account prior to an organisation setting strategic objectives.   **4**
   (b) Describe **3** tactical decisions that could lead to growth.   **3**

5. Lees' management use ratios to analyse financial data.
   (a) Describe ratios which could be used to ensure appropriate levels of profitability and liquidity are maintained.   **5**
   (b) Describe the limitations of using ratio analysis.   **3**

6. Lees changed the packaging of their products which made them more eye-catching and appealing to consumers.

   Explain **5** other methods of extending a product's life cycle.   **5**

7. Wholesalers buy goods in large quantities directly from manufacturers.

   Discuss the advantages and disadvantages to a manufacturer of using a wholesaler.   **5**

8. Discuss the role of appraisal and its ability to motivate staff.   **6**

     (50)

[END OF SECTION ONE]

SECTION TWO

Marks

This section should take you approximately 1 hour 15 minutes.

Answer TWO questions.

1. (a) Describe how both horizontal and vertical integration could allow an organisation to become even larger and more profitable.

   5

   (b) Describe methods a limited company could use to finance a successful takeover.

   4

   (c) Explain why firms use loss leaders as a pricing tactic.

   3

   (d) Describe the methods available to a Public Relations department to improve the image of an organisation.

   5

   (e) Many organisations group their activities by function.

   Discuss other methods an organisation could use to group their activities.

   8

   (25)

2. (a) Employees may undertake industrial action in an attempt to force employers to meet their demands.

   Describe types of industrial action that employees could take.

   4

   (b) Explain possible effects that prolonged industrial action could have on an organisation.

   5

   (c) (i) Distinguish between delayering and downsizing.

   3

   (ii) Explain the benefits to an organisation of using outsourcing.

   4

   (d) ICT is used to help head office communicate effectively with branches in remote areas of the country.

   Explain how modern technology can be used to communicate effectively within an organisation.

   6

   (e) Describe 3 types of production.

   3

   (25)

3. (a) Describe how stakeholders could make use of financial information provided by an organisation.

   7

   (b) Describe 4 causes of cash flow problems.

   4

   (c) (i) Identify and explain 3 economic factors that can affect the profitability of a business.

   6

   (ii) Describe 4 other external influences that can affect the success or failure of a business.

   4

   (d) Discuss the advantages and disadvantages to organisations such as Asda of selling own brand products.

   4

   (25)

[Turn over

Marks

SECTION TWO (continued)

4. (*a*) Organisations spend vast sums of money developing new products.

    Describe the stages that take place before a new product is launched onto the market.   **6**

    (*b*) Explain the advantages to an organisation of using market segmentation.   **4**

    (*c*) Explain the purpose of the Advertising Standards Authority.   **2**

    (*d*) (i) High quality and reliable information is essential if a manager is to make effective decisions.

    Describe the characteristics of high quality, reliable information.   **4**

    (ii) The Data Protection Act 1998 is the legislation which covers information stored on computers about individuals. Describe the main features of the Data Protection Act.   **5**

    (*e*) Explain the role of testing in the selection of new staff.   **4**

    (25)

5. (*a*) (i) Describe how the introduction of Quality Management (formerly TQM) techniques could ensure a quality product or service.   **5**

    (ii) Explain how the Human Resource Department can help to ensure that a quality product or service is produced.   **4**

    (*b*) (i) Describe the JIT stock control system.   **2**

    (ii) Describe the advantages and disadvantages of using such a system.   **5**

    (*c*) Describe how a manager could evaluate the effectiveness of a decision.   **4**

    (*d*) Describe the advantages and disadvantages of a wide span of control.   **5**

    (25)

[END OF QUESTION PAPER]

[BLANK PAGE]

[BLANK PAGE]

[BLANK PAGE]

[BLANK PAGE]